Use

What's Left

7 Strategies to Optimize Your

REBOUND

From Setback

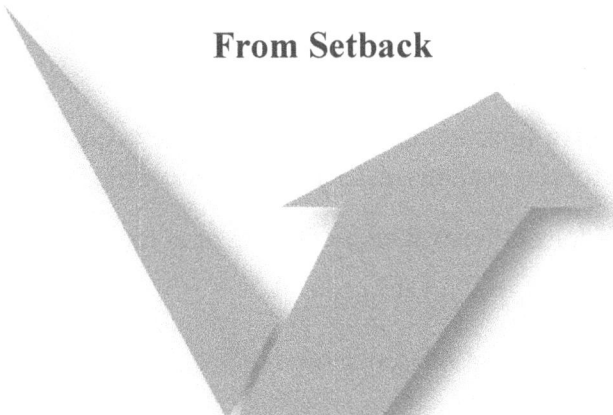

Dr. Ed Womack

Forward by Dr. Ruben West

Copyright Page

Contents

Acknowledgements

I wish to acknowledge all the many people who have made this book possible. This list is so long. I won't try and list everyone. There are people that are on the list that were only in my life for a season. Others have been here throughout my lifetime.

Each one of you have helped me not only recover, but also REBOUND to become the person I am today.

I sincerely want to thank you and publicly express my gratitude for your participation in the championship lifestyle I have been able to live. Every shot taken, every rebound, made a difference in my life and the lives of those I have touched and blessed. Know that you are loved, appreciated, and treasured.

Dr. Ed Womack

What's Left of Me?

Picking up pieces of you isn't easy,

When you never truly realized,

That you were broken in the first place,

Closed eyes and hidden lies.

I was a mess in my own disruption.

And when I realized I was sick,

It was hard to believe, I'd ever be

"Back from Broken."

Bruised skin and tattered clothes,

It was hard to see where I had fallen off,

But man, oh man, by the grace of God,

I am in a state of triumph.

I was far off the trail,

On which I needed to be,

And my heart was as shattered as glass,

And when I realized I was lost,

I saw the beginning of myself,

And a part of me was still in the past.

I had to move forward,

And realize my worth,

Because God had a plan in store,

He was picking me up and dusting me off.

Equipping me for something more,

Something bigger than myself, something greater than me,

Something I had never expected to see.

The beginning of myself, the restoration of a soul,

Using what was left of me.

Those pieces that had fallen off were not to go to waste,

They were to be used to bring me back in line,

Finally, on my feet and off the street,

The victory is finally mine.

Patricia J. Womack

Foreword

Dr. Ed Womack is no stranger to experience nor is he a stranger to bitterness. Life has taught him many lessons directly as a result of what he's been through. Having lost resources, time, and relationships to drugs, street life, and depression he found himself almost counted out by life. The good news is he decided to use what he had left.

According to Confucius, "By three methods we may learn wisdom: First, by reflection, which is noblest; second, by imitation, which is easiest; and third by experience, which is the bitterest." The question is, why is experience so bitter? Well, I believe it's because it takes something out of us.

Wouldn't it be great if we could go through life with the ability to maintain everything we started with? Imagine the possibilities for success if you never lost any of your money, never forfeited your time, and were able to easily maintain all of the things you thought were important. Unfortunately, you would never gain any experience or the wisdom that stems from it.

In this book, *Use What's Left*, Dr. Womack offers life-changing and relevant strategies gained from his many years of experience. He skillfully illustrates how life can resemble the game of basketball and how sometimes the best way to score is after a rebound. As I read this book it actually made me ponder some pointed questions: Have I been willing to reach for the rebound when I've been knocked down? Have I accepted my reality as inevitable, or instead, have I bounced back from life's setbacks to reach the height of true purpose that was within reach and fully available for me?

When I finished the first few chapters of *Use What's Left*, it was clear to me Dr. Womack was right in thinking he had more to give. By the time I finished reading the book, I discovered I had more to give as well! I believe you will have the same revelation as you digest the content of this work of art.

Each of the seven strategies eloquently and strategically presented reminded me of what it means to SCORE in life. Scoring goes beyond merely the setback or knock down. Scoring is taking strategic and intentional steps along with needed practice to win.

It's a given that you will have many opponents in life.

Furthermore, many of those opponents may be stronger, sharper, and/or smarter than you. But what's important is that if you stay the course and keep bouncing back from every setback, then you can not only SCORE, but get back in the game of life.

I have witnessed Dr. Ed Womack continue to work even when the odds were stacked against him. In that, I know a little bit of his background and his story and I see the championship lifestyle that he exhibits every day. Employing this type of resilience allows the rebounds, the scoring, and eventual winning to occur.

As you reach for the rebounds in your life, make sure you let these seven strategies become an integral part of your lifelong reality.

Will life knock you down? Yes! Will you have some losses? Yes! Will there be times when you are functioning with half the resources, half the time, and maybe even at half capacity? That very well could be. But here's what I know; when you find yourself in that difficult situation, don't throw in the towel. You can make it if you do what Dr. Womack suggests and that is to use what's left!

Ruben West, PhD

Preface

My life had been full of clichés. The whole "broke, busted and disgusted," "tore up from the floor up," "don't have a pot to piss in nor a window to throw it out of"—those were my go-to phrases. As I stood in downtown Decatur, Georgia, I had a moment of clarity during my pity party. I had been on crack for the last 18 months.

My drive to be self-destructive was starting to fade. I now just wanted to die slowly. Life was so negative that dying fast seemed too good for me. Just like those people across the street from me in the square. I sat on that concrete bench watching life. Not just life, but their lives, his life, her life, my life—all walking right past me. I could not move. I could not bring myself to walk across the street to the bright red pub with exposed brick on the side. There were people sitting out there on wooden barstools under green and white patio umbrellas. I remember being on the other side of the street. My place in life had changed. As I looked around me, I felt surrounded by nothingness.

It felt as though all my bad decisions surrounded me. My dreams behind me, my drug usage beside me and a bright red scarlet-letter-looking pub in front of me. I was hungry, I was tired, and I would not have minded a drink.

I just wanted to get myself together. Once, not long ago, I was the one enjoying food, imported beer and wine from the pub; now, I was just watching others living the life.

I, too, once had someone to smile at seated across from me at dinner. What do I have now? My life could have been compared to ants crawling on the ground. As I sat surrounded by my bad decisions, there were ants all around me. It was as if they mirrored my life.

Those ants were everywhere. You know the small, brown ants that pounce on a piece of bread by the hundreds? They looked like a brown, fuzzy ball. These ants are ever-present, but we don't notice them because of their relative insignificance.

Nobody cares about ants until they become a nuisance and hard to get rid of. In that moment, I wanted to take my foot and stomp on every one of them. I wanted to kill those ants, as they served no purpose to me either.

They were like scavengers on bread, climbing on top of each other for a little piece of pleasure. As crazy as it may sound, I found myself towering over those ants feeling powerful. How pathetic. The thought of crushing them seemed empowering.

And yet, I could relate to the responsibilities of those ants. They were so productive. They were lifting twice their body weight and providing for their dependents. They were dominating their environment. Those ants seemed like grown men.

Occasionally, I have had to carry the weight of others. This manifested itself in my family, work and community.

It appeared those little ants were oblivious to the potential danger that loomed above them. What creature would put itself out there for all to see, eat its meal, have leftovers and not fathom a dude like me could just stomp my large foot on them and it would be sudden death?

Not that those ants have emotions, but they operate on the premise that this is what they were destined and designed to do in order to survive.

They were willing to be seemingly suicidal every single day to carry out the cycle of life.

During this time, I felt as though I was not as brave as an ant. The sun was now blazing on my long-neglected face and I knew it was time to make a move.

I could not continue to sit there and stare at those ants. I had not showered in more than two weeks, smelled like 10 miles of hot garbage and I probably looked like a homeless person. I favored an image of what society may have called a crackhead. During that momentary haze, I had convinced myself I may be a "functioning crackhead." How absurd!

Would I be willing to expose myself in such a vulnerable manner as those ants, just for some food? No, but I could go sit among strangers and treat them as friends and family, knowing they just wanted to take my little piece of bread or whatever I had to give. I often found myself sitting in grungy, run-down buildings and hotels with chipped hardwood floors throughout the city of Decatur.

On that particular day those ants ignited a series of thoughts that required my immediate attention.

They were small, they were plentiful, and they were there for me to see; I just did not know *what I was supposed to feel. I desired to kill them and walk across the street.*

I wanted to pretend that the last 30-plus years of my life had not happened.

I wanted to awaken from the nightmare of the last year and a half of my life. The pain of not seeing my kids, or being able to take a hot steamy shower haunted me. The thought of fresh, clean linen pants to adorn my freshly oiled skin straight out the shower was something from the past.

I wanted every woman sitting under those green and white umbrellas to look at me across the road and say, "He's the MAN. He is the kind of man I want my guy to be. Here he comes, strong, bold, and ready to take care of his business and me." What business did I have? Well I didn't know.

All I could focus on were those ever-present ants. They were so brave to be out in the open like that. They didn't care if they died and I didn't care if I died either. I wanted those ants to die a slow death, as I felt I had been experiencing the last few years.

Bye-bye ants. After two steps toward the pub they were all dead. Just two steps caused their death. How many steps was it going to take for me to die? Fortunately, the ants were not the only things that would die that day. By the grace of God, so did the crackhead who had moved into my body.

On that November day of 2006 in downtown Decatur I experienced my death and birthday all in one. It was death to my crackhead ways and the renewal of my dreams and aspirations. The days characterized by gluttony, lying, cheating, drug use, deceiving others and myself died that day. Renewed dreams, aspirations, and potential began to start replacing the toxic thoughts and drugs that plagued my mind, spirit, and physical body.

The addiction to drugs was in the process of being replaced by a healthy obsession to wholeness and recovery. Who would have thought those itty-bitty brown ants would make such a big difference in my life?

Those ants provided a major breakthrough while I stood over them in deep thought. I was instantly inspired and motivated to discover how the cycle of life could be better. This further made me want to seek and discover what "purpose" really meant. Life began to take on a very different perspective; the mirror of self was now starting to take form and shape again. The rehabilitation of my self-image had a long way to go but the true rehabilitation — the rehabilitation of self-reflection — had begun.

I could no longer look into empty storefront windows to see my reflection. Many times, there was nothing looking back at me anyways. I now wanted to see myself when I looked into a mirror or window. Not my old self, or my new self, just who I was destined to be.

I looked all over for me. I looked in the streets, at the bottom of bottles, at the bottom of dope baggies, at the bottom of stairs, at the bottom of broken promises and rich lies. I looked for me in other people, places, and things, and wondered why I couldn't find me. I looked for me in mind- and mood-altering substances that were designed to destroy me and all who ventured to use them.

All those things, those vices, those excuses happened to me every day. Just not that day! That day I killed those ants with the same feet I used to walk across the square in an attempt to find me— the "me" that was always there but I could not find before.

That day I saw him. The other guy was dead and only I existed. Whoever "I" is, we would have to get to know each other all over again. I welcomed that. It had been years since I welcomed change, death and rebirth. It was now time for my renewal and reinvention.

In my first book, Back from Broken, *I began sharing my true-life story. During that transparent and therapeutic book, I shared how I went from what appeared to be the top of the game of life to the bottom in a very short period of time.*

It is my distinct pleasure to share with you now my seven strategies to optimize your rebound.

In life, many of us can attest to the fact at some time or another, we have all been dealt a difficult hand to play. The ability to rebound from a setback is the premise for the writings you are about to read. In Back from Broken, *I shared the many life experiences I was exposed to that left me broken.*

In my opinion, the most unjustifiable parts of being broken is one, not knowing you are broken, and two, not knowing how to bounce back or be resilient when you are in that broken state. There is, however, a process to getting up from that place and I like to call it the REBOUND.

As a broken individual, you may feel like there is nothing left that can help you get to that place where you are able to function, move forward, and start rebuilding those things that have been broken in your life. You realize you are stuck in a wounded state, with fragments of painful experiences, a jaded identity, and a broken life. In the writings of this book, I share specific strategies that helped me to come back from broken and assisted me in now being able to use what's left."

My hope for you is that as you share this journey and read, you too will be able to use these strategies and find the keys to assist you in the process of moving forward on your journey.

Using what's left will definitely help you make the REBOUND and not only will you rebound, you will win!

As the Urban Leadership Strategist, I am equipped to show you how to apply these strategies that when used properly will help you win repeatedly. There is a champion within you, and no matter how broken you have been, you too can succeed!

Dr. Ed Womack

Seven Strategies To Optimize Your REBOUND

In the book, I will discuss in detail the seven strategies to completing a rebound. These strategies are proven techniques that helped me recover from a place where I almost lost hope and my life.

These seven simple strategies, if followed correctly will lead to success in your life. REBOUND is an acronym. Below are the modules of the REBOUND methodology:

R = Reinvent Yourself

E = Extend and Excel

B = Bake It, Don't Microwave It

O = Optimize Opportunities

U = Understanding Births Knowledge

N = Negate Negativity

D = Demand Your Destiny

In this book, we will explore each of the modules of the REBOUND methodology to help you make a successful rebound in any area of life you're currently struggling with. Often, we may need to end addiction, relationships and circumstances that are holding us back from being the best we can and were designed to be.

Sometimes a REBOUND is necessary to bring us back from the place of being broken and up to the place of blessing. That's what this book is all about: achieving the ultimate REBOUND that turns your life around and redirects it for success and reaching the goals you desire for your life.

The strategies laid out here, when followed consistently, will lead to significant preparation to win in your relationships, community, and the world at large. This will be in accordance to the purpose that has been waiting for you. It's your time to be restored, understood, and respected—despite the trauma, setbacks, poor decisions, or other mishaps.

R

Faith is taking the first step even when you don't
see the whole staircase.
— Dr. Martin Luther King Jr.

Reinvent Yourself

L et's start with the module of reinventing yourself. This module encompasses several characteristics of recreating your habits by facing some personal truths. There is a saying the truth will set you free, but it can't set you free until you face the lies that are holding you hostage. I have created five steps to begin the process of reinventing one's self.

- Admit there is a problem
- Peel back the layers
- Let your guard down
- Prayer and meditation
- Affirmations

Admitting and/or acknowledging there is room for improvement is the first step in making an active change in your life. You can't fix a problem you refuse to acknowledge. An unacknowledged problem is like an infection that has not been discovered in the body. If not properly treated, it could turn into a deadly situation. When I approached adulthood and left home, the issues I felt I was escaping were not being dealt with. I merely hid them and acted as if they did not affect me.

As time went on, those issues I thought I ran away from caught up with me and lead me down a path that was choking the life out of me. I didn't want to live; I just wanted to hide from the world. I used mind- and mood-altering substances to try and hide from myself and those that encountered me. With each high I was pushed deeper into that fake hiding place. Once I acknowledged I had unresolved issues, I had to face them to begin the process of healing.

The "peel back the layers" step can be a painful rung on the ladder on the pathway to reinventing one's self. It can be like peeling the layers of an onion. Tears may often accompany this reflection. I had years of heartbreaking situations that were difficult for me to face. Although it evoked many emotions and caused some forms of anger, bitterness, and resentment, I had to get through every layer of the pain to truly start healing. For some, it may cause the shedding of tears, but it is there that cleansing and true healing can begin.

On the outside I looked strong and confident, but on the inside, I was at war with my warped perceptions and the reality that loomed around me.

In my moments of reflection, I realized my life had become unmanageable, reeking with an odor that made the results stink. Each layer represented the times I did what I thought kept me insulated from the pain, but in actuality it was the very cause of my discomfort.

Once I admitted there was room for improvement, I could see the harm my prior choices had caused me. It was then that I was ready to peel back the layers and make steps toward a life of positive change and healing.

The next critical step in reinventing one's self is to "let your guard down." This means to allow yourself to first, peel back the layers, and second, to admit there is a problem.

This step is most likely going to be different for men and women.

Men are less likely to want to show emotion in this step. As a young man, I dealt with the most violating experience a man could ever encounter. Someone close to me was the violator of my trust. This was the cause for a deep-seated inability to trust others. In other words, I had trust issues. This of course made me become guarded of my emotions, expressions and willingness to seek help in *anything*.

How could I allow anyone into my most intimate space, and be open enough to let the healing I so needed begin to occur? I did this by following the previous steps. In the times I was being violated, my young mind didn't know how to process what was being done. I kept silent, never allowing that information to escape. I held it in for years and like a cancer it ate away at my core being.

Men, please know you can be vulnerable enough in this process to speak about the thing that is causing you the greatest pain. Be careful to only share with a nonjudgmental, caring, and supportive individual. Your life is on the line and in order to fully rebound, you have to be willing to be vulnerable. In this process, it is imperative to have a team you can trust, a team that fully supports you when you let down the guardrails around your heart.

It can be challenging, but it is absolutely necessary to make sure you get the most out of your support team. This team of individuals can provide a safe zone for you where your vulnerability will not be mishandled or abused.

I found my first team of supporters at Trinity House. This was the place where my rebound began. I was able to face my truth head-on in a safe zone of healing and recovery. It wasn't a comfortable process, but it afforded me the time and clarity to begin. I had to be willing to take the defense mechanism down and allow the healing power of truth to take place.

The next step in this process is understanding the power of prayer and meditation are crucial components to assure success. I believe it comes first in these five steps even though it is listed as the fourth step. Prayer to a Higher Authority connects us to the source of who we truly are. We are connected to our Creator through prayer. Prayer is even more powerful when we still the mind in meditation and allow our Creator to speak to us. In the quiet time is where we get clarity on the steps and progress we are making in our lives.

Meditation is also a way to help us focus on the issues we wish to bring the change we desire. In the Bible, David meditated on the promises of God, which helped him overcome the craziness that was happening in his life because of the bad choices he had made. Even in his bad choices he was still a chosen king. Through the power of meditation and prayer he was empowered to rebuild when he was torn down, and it also enabled him to never forget who God said he was. Prayer and meditation keeps us centered and connected with our Creator, and is one of the most pertinent factors in these five steps.

Affirmations are written and spoken declarations. It is said life and death are in the power of the tongue (Proverbs 18:21). Affirmations enable us to create life with our spoken words. Words are the invaluable tools we use to communicate with each other and with ourselves. We can be cautiously aware of what we say to others, but I admonish you to be more aware of what you say to yourself.

Oftentimes we may think what others say to us could be life-changing, and it can be; but even more so what comes from our own lips is what cripples us the most. Affirm what the Creator has said about who you are until you see what your Creator has said about you and experience it come to life.

Using affirmations help to create the positive energy needed to reinvent yourself. Speaking affirmations every morning after prayer and meditation consistently can create a massive change in one's paradigm and belief system.

You will discover that for these activities to be effective, they must be done consistently and over a continuous period of time. In this time frame, one can set a new paradigm and create new habits.

According to research from Maxwell Maltz, who was a plastic surgeon in the 1950s, he began noticing a pattern among his patients.

When Dr. Maltz would operate on a patient, he found it would take the person about 21 days to adjust—to a new face after a nose job, or to stop sensing a missing limb after an amputation.

Maltz reflected on his own adjustment period to changes and new behaviors, and found it also took him about 21 days to form a new habit. Maltz wrote about these experiences in his book *Psycho-Cybernetics*, and said, "These, and many other commonly observed phenomena tend to show that it requires a minimum of about 21 days for an old mental image to dissolve and a new one to jell."

Reinvention, much like the insight from Maltz above, needs to take place continuously to change a habit or set a new one.

However, it is my estimation that it takes closer to 90 days to create a new habit fully and make it an irreversible part of one's new self. Even after 90 days, I believe a person must continue to practice this process because some habits are very hard to break. The main component in changing habits is making a daily and intentional commitment to become a better you each and every day.

Hilary Rettig, the author of *The 7 Secrets of the Prolific*, highlights mornings as setting the tone for a good or bad day.

"For many people, the morning holds our freshest, most energetic hours," Rettig says. "Good time managers value ever smaller amounts of time. Those first few minutes of your day—both at home and when you get to the office—are vital."

This suggests the first 15 minutes of each day shapes and defines the results one can expect to see manifest in their life, work, and play. It sets the tone and positions you to face that new day with confidence, conviction and courage. In those first 15 minutes, there should be meditation, prayer, and spoken affirmations.

These affirmations should be spoken as if you were cheering on your favorite sports team. The energy you use to cheer yourself on should always be high! As your coach, I encourage you to believe in yourself and the power that your Creator has given you.

Each of these activities allows you to zero in on the thing that is the focus of your future. It creates a positive flow for you to clear your mind, to affirm, and develop a mindset conducive for reaching the goals you set.

The mind is the breeding ground for all success. It all starts in your mind. According to the wisdom-filled words of Henry Ford: "If you think you can, or you think you can't, you are probably right." Tell yourself repeatedly about the power you possess to create the life you desire. If you didn't know, let me be the first to tell you that you can create the exact life you desire to live. Following these steps in this book helped me to go from a place of extreme brokenness to a place of empowerment!

You must ask yourself, how can I do better today than I did yesterday? What will be the continuous movement to take me from where I am to where I want to be? These are the questions that someone in the process of personal reinvention must ask themselves.

The five steps in this module are some of the tools needed to create the *new* you.

Pride and fear will try to come in and hinder your progress. However, with consistent application of these five steps, you can make successful strides in reinventing yourself.

Steps to Score

When you Reinvent Yourself

1. Improve one thing daily.
2. Meditate daily for 15 minutes.
3. Do a random act of kindness daily.
4. Encourage others in their purpose daily.
5. Write down your dreams and goals.
6. Read inspirational/motivational content daily.
7. Shift your thoughts from negative to positive daily.
8. Prepare and pursue your purpose daily.
9. Try something new to stretch yourself daily.
10. Surround yourself with positive and supportive people regularly.

E

Good is the enemy of Great.
—Jim Collins

Extend and Excel

As a starting player on the high school varsity basketball team, I learned a lot about rebounding. We were not just any high school basketball team; we were one of the elite teams in the state of Michigan and one of the best in the city of Detroit. As basketball players, it was necessary to stretch, extend and to push us to excellence, because our goal was to win a state championship. This was critical for each player, and our coach.

In the year that we achieved that distinction we were undefeated. We went 27-0 against some very tough and talented teams throughout the state. You might want to ask yourself, what was the focus and motivation that allowed us to achieve such an incredible feat? It began with us extending and pushing ourselves beyond our known limits. We began to envision and thirst for a season of exceeding the ordinary. We were collectively destined to achieve excellence.

Excellence doesn't simply occur unless you intentionally extend yourself to acquire it.

One of the ways we began to extend ourselves was to have "super practices." These were two practices a day that were grueling and highly intensive both physically and mentally. They not only required shooting, passing, dribbling, and rebounding, but also running and physical endurance training. On some days we would even have film sessions to allow us to get the mental edge on our opponents. We frequently left the super practices tired and worn out. We watched videos and tapes of all our opponents and got to know their tendencies and skill sets well. In an effort to maintain stamina and conditioning, year-round, each player had to do something aside from our first love of basketball during the off-season and it was mandatory. I found myself running cross-country as a means of building my stamina off-season.

We didn't enjoy the process of extending ourselves in this manner. However, if we hadn't endured those super practice sessions, we would've allowed ourselves to become defeated by fatigue and other issues beyond our control. As I previously stated, we faced great teams, but we were greater because we were better prepared. To REBOUND and win you must push yourself. A person must face difficulty to excel beyond the comfort zone. Life is like a muscle—if it is not worked out, stretched, and pushed, it will become dormant and lose tone. It becomes useless.

As you consider what is needed to extend and excel, to consciously and intentionally get better, you must stretch beyond your comfort zone.

An important thing to understand and consider is that success occurs outside of what we feel most comfortable with. If there is no growth inside the comfort zone some may think it's an okay place to be. The amazing Dr. Clarice Fluid once said, "Champions perform differently than other folks." Champions live outside the comfort zone. To extend and excel means you are willing to do the hard work that no one else is willing to do. Extending is doing the uncomfortable work so that you can excel at whatever it is you are working on. One must be committed to this process if they plan to win at their life, work or play.

Another favorite quote of mine from Dr. Martin Luther King was: "Faith is taking the first step even when you don't see the entire staircase." You must have a goal to extend yourself and do your very best if you expect to attain excellence.

The willingness to go beyond your known and unknown limitations allows you to exceed expectations and eventually arrive at excellence. Push yourself even if it means going outside of your previously embraced areas of ease. There was a time in my life when I made the choice to be comfortable instead of growing. I chose to be comfortable living beneath my ability, and it resorted to the use of various mind- and mood-altering substances, people and things to pacify the pain, all because I didn't want to face the underlying realities of my past.

In the past, instead of working to be a loving, caring and compassionate husband, I would delve into my work, sports, or anything that would not force me to put in the needed effort of being a husband. I can remember reducing the marriage to simply a "relationship of convenience." I took what I called the "chicken exit," because it was easy to ignore or omit, rather than commit and improve. I spiraled down to my detriment because I became satisfied with what I thought was comfort. At that moment of disarray, it was a cancer that gobbled up my life and spit out a monster I did not know. Choosing not to grow is equal to choosing to die a slow and painful death. Growth is a vital part of life.

While extending yourself to grow, there may be some pain in the process but the beauty behind that pain is priceless.

If trees or plants are to grow they must *pruned*. The definition of pruning is: trimming (a tree, shrub, or bush) by cutting away dead or overgrown branches or stems, especially to increase fruitfulness and growth.

I think it is necessary for you and me to be pruned in different areas in our lives as well.

We rarely like situations that are not the norm for us. We tend to dislike the pressure that life presents to us on occasion as well. I think we can learn a lot from the process that creates diamonds. There is great pressure in the earth's core in order for diamonds to formulate. That pressure serves a purpose. That pressure is required to birth the magnificence of the diamond for all to see. When you allow the pressure to serve you, and not stop you, then you understand the significance of moving out of your comfort zone and evolving into your own amazingness.

The programming from our childhood can form some limiting beliefs that can make this module difficult. For example, when we were children in elementary school, we had to raise our hands first to be able to speak. This was a good lesson that taught children how to speak one at a time. However, as an adult, that lesson can become somewhat limiting. Some of us are still raising our hands to speak, or seeking approval to be the person we desire to be. We are raising our hand because we want the acknowledgement that it is okay to become the great person we were destined to be.

We pause if we don't receive permission to speak. What are you pausing and looking for permission to do in your life now? The lessons taught to us early in life are what formed our paradigm or our belief system. That paradigm can create a resistance to pushing past your comfort zone as well as enhance the limiting beliefs that hinder many from achieving their maximum level of excellence. Too many people accept it because it has been programmed into them all their lives and it is all they know.

To REBOUND is to go beyond that past programming. To REBOUND is to push forward toward excellence. The undisputed top bestseller of all times, the Bible says, "When I was a child I spoke as a child, I thought and understood as a child, behaved as a child, but when I became a man I put aside childish things" (1 Corinthians 13:11).

You may relate to childishness as being something negative, but this childishness simply means the acts of a child. At some point in life you have to grow up and perform the *adult* lessons that you have learned. Don't be afraid to apply what you have learned. Once you apply what you have learned then this will be where you begin to excel. You may have felt stuck or felt like you had nothing to offer, but you could not be more wrong.

If you had nothing to offer you would have not been created. The Creator made all things for a purpose. Nothing is made without a reason. Nobody can fulfill your purpose but you! You are a special design and the gift the Creator gave you to share with the world is important. At first, I wasn't the best at basketball, but I extended myself. I challenged myself and eventually I became the best! Extending yourself happens on a mental level first and then the actions are carried out physically because you have decided to excel and achieve all that you were designed to be. Will challenges come? Yes, but you must decide to push through anything that hinders you. When you build that determination to succeed, nothing will stop you.

Having made many poor choices, I had to dedicate myself to use the "extend and excel" strategy of the REBOUND methodology to begin to excel in life.

I was delivered from drugs, delusion, and depression. This process happened over time, yet it only occurred because I was ready to REBOUND. Part of that process began when I made the decision to extend myself past the barriers that limited me, and I began to operate in excellence. You must extend and reach for excellence if you are to achieve anything in life.

Those who haven't committed to anything great can't extend themselves. Mediocrity requires no great push. It requires nothing extraordinary of anyone. If your choice is to live and walk in excellence you must be willing to be uncomfortable.

Greatness and excellence takes consistent effort. It takes pushing beyond where you are and who you are. Believe and see yourself elevated past the current place where you may be.

Extend yourself daily so you can rebound from trials, tests and situations that can stop and overwhelm the average person.

If you are willing to extend yourself, then you are destined to excel. You must make a habit of great expectation, tenacious pursuit, and constantly prepare yourself daily for greatness. It must become a part of your DNA. Choose to extend in the midst of the trials and difficult circumstances. Once you create the habit of extending, then you will build the courage and discipline it takes to excel.

One very important fact to observe when implementing the strategy of this module is to know you can't continue doing the same thing expecting a different result. To continue doing this would be classified as being insane. This module will help you to stop the insanity by stepping outside your comfort zone, doing the hard work and building the strength and courage to excel in every capacity.

Steps to Score
When you Extend and Excel

1. Commit to your new vision and goals.

2. Do something you have never imagined or done.

3. Seek out coaches and mentors in your field of interest.

4. Use past failures to advance your learning.

5. Don't compromise your dreams and goals for naysayers.

6. Laser focus on your niche and own it.

7. Read educational industry specific content daily.

8. Eliminate excuses and accept your life.

9. Execute your purpose, despite your fears.

10. Find yourself a skilled circle of people who have influence.

B

Patience, persistence, and perspiration make
an unbeatable combination for success.
—Napoleon Hill

Bake It! Don't Microwave It!

Baking is kindred to patience. The definition of patience is the capacity to accept or tolerate delay, trouble, or suffering without getting angry or upset.

This module is vitally important. Most who read it may not immediately embrace it. Especially in this hurry up, instant gratification, "I want it yesterday" world we live in today. Many are not fond of allowing the natural course of *process* to occur. Everything in life has a process.

Have you ever found yourself thinking back to some of the situations and encounters of your past and wonder Why me? Why now? How did I end up here? How did I make this same mistake again?

In this world of instant gratification, we can sometimes overlook the importance and necessity of the journey. There are no shortcuts en route to your REBOUND. I often use the analogy of baking an apple pie crust to illustrate the context of the difference between baking and microwaving. Even if you get all your ingredients right and instead of baking it in the oven, you decide to toss it in the microwave, chances are you will not get the ideal or desired result. The microwaved crust would have a totally different texture than the one you bake. The taste would also be less desirable.

When we attempt to shortcut the proper method of preparation, just like that microwaved piecrust, we fall apart. Attempting to speed up the time it takes to complete the creation will typically compromise the desired end result.

Another analogy would be Granny's banana pudding. It was made from scratch, and I got so excited every time she started to make it because I knew it was going to be delicious! She would get the freshest ingredients and lay them out all on the table in sequence. I loved to sit there and watch her make it. Just as I have laid the steps out to implement the rebound in your life, my Granny laid out the ingredients she was going to use. She knew everything had to be added in the correct sequence. She realized if she missed an ingredient the pudding that resulted would not be her best!

When we face our personal challenges along this journey called life, we have to push through the obstacles. We must stop and take the necessary time, energy, and perseverance required to succeed.

Baking is a craft where you have the task of following specific directions to ensure the final product tickles the tummy of all who taste it. Baking gives exact measurements of the ingredients that will be used because too much or too little of any ingredient will alter the results. When you attempt to shortcut the process of the REBOUND you will alter the results of your life. Let's be honest; how many of you have started a diet and it didn't work? Well I can tell you for sure, it's not the diet.

Oftentimes we mess up when there is a comparison of the results between the people following the diet and those who don't. Jane may lose five pounds in two weeks, but John may lose 10 pounds in two weeks. Jane concludes that the diet is not working for her because John lost more weight. There is another conclusion. Instead of Jane celebrating her weight loss, she gave up because she compared herself to John. However, we don't always get through the process at the same rate of time. That does not mean you have made no progress at all. Slow progress is always better than no progress, and just because we do not progress the same way as others does not mean we are not moving forward in the best way for ourselves.

Granny always took her time making the banana pudding. She would use only the purest vanilla extract, Chiquita bananas, and Nilla brand vanilla wafers. That brand was mandatory to get the optimal taste she wanted. Granny used nothing but the best ingredients for her recipes. Sugar, butter, and all the other ingredients were laid out on the counter. After all of that, I would get to lick the bowl, which was one of my favorite highlights in the preparation process. I would always ask, "Granny is it done yet, is it done yet?"

She would always say, "Not yet baby, but it's almost done." That anticipation and expectation is what kept me going and kept me waiting. I would walk by and the most wonderful smell would hit me. I just couldn't wait to taste one of Granny's best recipes. However, I had to wait patiently because the process had to take its time.

Today we want everything right now! Walking toward excellence is not an overnight journey. Success takes time and once you have followed the correct path, it yields great results.

Contrary to the common desire of today to have things happen immediately, the steps required to assure an effective and long-lasting REBOUND. sometimes require us to look to our *mental spice rack*. On a well-stocked mental spice rack, we find ingredients such as patience, persistence, humility, courage, wise counsel, mentoring, and coaching. These ingredients should be measured and mixed into our daily lives very carefully.

We may find that as we begin to combine the items gathered from our mental spice rack, unforeseen changes in temperature may be needed to overcome the trials, obstacles, setbacks, and even failures that are guaranteed to find themselves in the mix of our lives at some point or another.

The environment we are born into, nurtured by as we grow, and the choices we make either knowingly or uninformed, will also dictate the proper mixing of ingredients needed and the correct temperatures to be used.

Between the ages of five and 50 we have our minds programmed with many things we have learned, some of them correctly, some of them incorrectly. Mileage and maturity will definitely play a key role in what our unique "baking" process will look like. Just like the various tasty dishes Granny would prepare, each dish has a particular recipe.

Let's be very clear, the "Bake It, Don't Microwave It" strategy could take hours, days, and sometimes months or years to reverse life-long programming we may be faced with at the time we commit to "use what's left" to optimize our respective REBOUND.

For example, if a person has used a mind- or mood-altering substance for 10 years, been subjected to abuse and rejection, overwhelmed by life without the proper ingredients that life requires, there wouldn't be an immediate change in that person once they commit to "Bake It, Don't Microwave It."

We should never give up on our attempt to REBOUND, no matter how long it takes.

This is not to say a miraculous change is not possible. However, long-lasting, effective change takes time. Never give up, because the desired results don't happen as fast as you may think.

Today, many people want the microwave results. First, you must ask yourself, what type of results will you receive following the microwave method? Secondly, will your results be long-lasting?

When a house is built, the ground where the house will stand must be tested to see if it can hold the weight of the house. If the ground is not tested the foundation may not be strong enough to stand the test of time.

The journey to *Use What's Left* is essential, and you will see how much better off you will become by following the "Bake It Don't Microwave It" modality. Taking shortcuts diminishes the level of success you will see in your pursuit to rebound from whatever setback you may have to overcome.

Discipline and consistency are key once you begin to change and "use what's left."

Above all, you must remember that anything worth having is worth working hard for. The "baking" may seem tedious, unnecessary, and even exhausting at times, but you will grow and find new ways to create a delicious looking and tasting life for yourself.

When we look at the skill of a baker, or someone like my Grandma, you may think the skills came very easily to them. Granny learned over the years from her mother and other family members that following the process will give you a better chance of becoming successful. That dedication allowed Granny to make wonderful tasting desserts. She had to have a teacher (coach), to show her how to choose the right ingredients, and put those ingredients together properly to produce the result she desired.

If Granny as a young lady decided to override or shortcut the process, her cake wouldn't taste the same as her mother's cake. As in life, when we have been given specific directions to follow and don't execute those directions as expected, the results will not be the same as predicted by our coaches or mentors.

When following a plan created for success, some may say after trying it for a period of time that it doesn't work. A plan won't work if you don't work the plan. The plan is only a guideline to direct you. Taking the proper time to follow the directions of the plan is all on you.

It is understandable that some people may want fast results when presented with challenges because nobody likes to feel the pain of being down and out.

Please recognize it took time to get down and it will take time to get up. As an athlete, you don't start off being the best on the team; it takes time and practice to develop and sharpen your skills. Even the most talented player must practice. The coach is there to guide the players through their plan to become the best athlete possible. The coach knows each player must be trained, developed, and equipped for the challenge of the game.

The coach is there to help you learn and give you guidance on how to take your best shot, or in Grandma's case, make the best cake. In the world today, perhaps better known as the microwave age, we may think doing more in a short period of time will produce the same quality outcome as taking our time to allow the process to work slowly and successfully.

There is something very powerful to be discovered when you begin to realize the power of and purpose for the journey. You will realize that just as a tea bag, you don't know how strong you really are until you are put in hot water. Today I challenge you to discover how strong you are and build the endurance needed to get you to the next level of your REBOUND. Anything that is built to last has gone through a rigorous process. The process is not about getting it right all the time, the process is about staying the course.

Everyone has messed up at some time or another, even Granny, but she didn't stop baking because of a couple of failures. You may have to start all over on occasion. Do not be discouraged and know sometimes the time spent in our "valley" moments, or low points in life, are where some real growth and development occur if we faint not and keep going!

Believe it or not, failures can and will help you get better and better if you stay dedicated to the process.

In my book, *Back from Broken*, I share all about being in the most vulnerable place in my life mentally and spiritually. When I made the decision to change my life and enter the Trinity House Program I knew then the baking process was going to last well beyond overnight. I took a two-year break from life so that I could be the person you see today. In the process of my healing, I didn't rush it. It had taken time to get me down in the dumps, so it was going to take time to lift me up. Not just time but concentrated and focused time, energy, patience, humility, frustration, persistence, failure, and disappointments along the way.

While a resident at the Trinity House I was able take advantage of the journey to success that they had developed. I followed the recipe for success intently and here I am standing as living proof that the "baking" process is not to break you but to make you better. Had I been defiant and wanted to take a shortcut, I would have risked a chance of falling apart just like the piecrust in the microwave. I encourage you to value yourself enough to endure the process. The results will definitely be rewarding!

You will discover when you take your time and don't rush things the result is something to not only be cherished but expected. The microwave mindset says rush it and just get it done. The bake it mindset suggests, when you follow the order of things, and allow for time, the results will be worth the wait.

Steps to Score

When you Bake It Don't Microwave It

1. Commit to your new vision and goals.

2. Realize your goals require time and effort.

3. Stay the course even when setbacks occur.

4. Share wins and losses with coaches and mentors.

5. Shy away from silver bullet thinking.

6. Don't set unreasonable expectations for yourself.

7. Take time to reflect and adjust periodically.

8. Resist hasty decisions when under pressure.

9. Realize there is pleasure in the journey.

10. Work smart to prevent burnout.

O

"The opportunity of a lifetime needs to be seized during the lifetime of the opportunity."

— Leonard Ravenhill

Optimize Opportunities

The definition of *optimize* is to make the best or most effective use of something. In this module, we focus on optimizing opportunity. When facing a setback, there seems to be few opportunities. You may find yourself lacking vision, having no aspirations, and feeling there is no end to the current frustrations. One may say they don't have many resources to work with after facing a challenge. Rock bottom is a place where many feel there is nothing there that can help them.

You may feel that all the opportunities have been depleted, but in the words of the amazing Les Brown, "If you can look up, you can get up." This is where I implore you to "use what's left." You may feel you lack resources, but the resources are plentiful. It is the resourcefulness that you may lack. Opportunities can often elude you when you don't see them because of a lack of vision to even believe there is a chance to receive an opportunity.

Also, having an opportunity without the wisdom on how to optimize it can have you at a standstill. There is a quote that reads: "The eyes are useless if the mind is blind." -Unknown Vision is required to optimize any opportunity. You need to see it through your eyes both mentally and physically. Having this vision helps you to evaluate the opportunities around you and make a wise decision whether this opportunity will push you closer to your goals or pull you away.

My mentor, Dr. Ruben West, stated in a training module, "You have to take advantage of an opportunity of a lifetime within the lifetime of the opportunity." Don't allow feelings of inadequacy to keep you stagnant and prevent you from acting on the opportunities you are presented with. Optimizing those opportunities allows you to take advantage of and gain the wisdom needed to use what is available to you at that time.

The opportunities you fail to use can become another person's opportunity if you don't recognize it, or didn't make the best of the opportunity when it came to you. The ability to recognize the unlimited opportunities available to you is also an important factor in optimizing an opportunity. Have you ever felt stuck in a bad circumstance? When facing a setback, a feeling of lost hope can set in and if you're not careful it can blind you mentally from seeing the opportunities that may be available. Your mental receptors must be able to recognize opportunities made available to you.

When I began to walk in the path of my destiny I had to find the opportunity to become more proficient in the work I was doing. Having very little experience in being a motivational speaker, I sought out those individuals who I respected and had a lot of success in that discipline. I had to place myself in an environment that provided opportunities. When I was rebounding from my setback I knew I had to find those that could help me grow. Previously, those opportunities were not available to me. I made the decision to change my circle of influencers. Dr. Dennis Kimbro stated, "If you're the smartest person in the room, you may want to find a different room." If you're looking to get rich then emulate rich people; if you want to amass wealth then emulate wealthy people; if you want to become excellent, then emulate excellent people. In order to emulate these individuals, it begins with surrounding yourself with these individuals. Do exactly what they do. If you are never around successful people to emulate, then there is a low chance of achieving that goal. Your circle of influence needs to be one that can guide you to the desired path of growth and full of opportunity.

You may say: "I don't really know any successful people personally." Well, allow me to share one true story with you. My desire was to become an active motivational speaker. I wanted to be able to change lives. I was always the technical guy, so using the internet I saw a video of a man standing on stage who was a well-known motivational speaker, Les Brown, in South Africa. I decided to contact the guy I saw on stage with Les Brown.

Now being transparent, I didn't expect to get a call back from this man. To my surprise, I received a call in two days! He is now my personal mentor, Dr. West. Now, what made me have the courage to reach out to Dr. West and ask him for his guidance? What made me feel I was qualified enough to be in the company of the likes of Les Brown and Ruben West? It was my decision to grow and optimize every opportunity that came my way.

Let me be honest and say that yes, fear may enter your thoughts, but you must overcome that fear and *stinking thinking*. Stinking thinking is the insane, totally illogical, irrational thoughts one may allow to permeate and control the majority of their thinking. The good news is you can change that stinking thinking at any time you chose by simply making another choice. Make a choice to be courageous in pursuit of your goals and development.

This is just one example of taking advantage of an opportunity to connect with someone who was in the position to help me reach the goal to become a life-changing speaker. Had I allowed my fear to stop me, I would have never positioned myself to make the best of the opportunity that presented itself to me.

There are two analogies regarding fear that I want you to think about. These analogies will help you make the choice that will help you propel forward or shrink backward. You can either forget everything and run, or face everything and rise. I want you to remember that you can *rise*. Fear doesn't have to limit you. Fear can be the emotion to push you forward.

Always be aware and alert of these opportunities. Keep in mind you are not the only one looking to optimize their opportunities. Your opportunities might manifest themselves as cooking delectable meals, creating and performing mellowing melodies via a musical instrument or your voice. Perhaps you may have the gift of attentive listening when others need to be heard instead of lectured to. The point here is that we all have unique gifts, talents and abilities. The late Dr. Myles Munroe said it best: "Your gift will make room for you."

Never allow the focus on what you don't have to override the focus on what you do have. As I stated before, I wasn't the best shooter on the basketball team in high school, but I didn't quit just because I wasn't the best at shooting. I eventually became the best. That is an honest example on how to optimize an opportunity.

Optimize situations that will focus on your unique skills, talents, and abilities. While on my high school basketball team I realized I didn't have to be the best shooter to be an asset to my team. My opportunity was just being on the team. I could have made the choice to just settle on being a benchwarmer because my shooting skills were not good, or I could have decided to practice more and more until my skills matched my will. Great achievers can move through obstacles that may try to hinder their progress by first having the drive to achieve.

You must have determination to make the best of every opportunity presented to you. Making the best of opportunities, I made sure I learned everything to make my skill set grow and expand. Another important factor in this module is perspective. Perspective helped me see myself in a different light. Perspective helped me to see myself not as a failure but as a person who was on a journey to achieve greatness. Wayne Dyer said, "If you change the way you look at things, the things you look at will change." This quote helped me change the way I saw my situations and circumstances. It gave me the power to move forward simply by changing my perspective.

At this phase you may have the mindset to have a clear path before proceeding toward my set goals. In other words, you may want to have everything right before you optimize the opportunity. Let me encourage you with this statement: You don't have to be great to get started, but you do have to get started to be great. Start where you are, regardless of where you may or may not believe that should be, then "optimize the opportunities."

Steps to Score
When you Optimize Opportunity

1. Strategically network with the masterminds of your field.

2. Don't be distracted; be attracted to new endeavors.

3. Resist telling people how to help you.

4. Realize done is better than perfect.

5. Run with the winners, not the whiners.

6. Invite your coach/mentor to evaluate your performance.

7. Evaluate your inner circle of influence for constructive feedback.

8. Invest and learn at the level you expect to earn.

9. Don't get busy confused with productive.

10. Take time to reflect and adjust periodically.

U

Seek first to understand, then to be understood.

—Stephen Covey

Understanding Births Knowledge

In this module, we will take a look at the importance of gaining understanding. In the Bible, we are told in a proverb from King Solomonthat "Wisdom isthe principal thing, therefore get wisdom; and in all thy getting get understanding" (Proverbs 4:7). Even in attaining wisdom there is a process. As we journey through the REBOUNDyou will see how each lesson connects. As I created these lessons, I always gave respect to the process.

Wisdom births understanding. Understanding births knowledge. Author Stephen Covey stated in one of the habits in the book *Seven Habits of Highly Effective People*, that we should "seek first to understand." When processing a setback sometimes we must look back to understand just how we got there.

Once we look back and understand how we got there in the first place, there will be lessons to be gained from the past experiences.

These past experiences when viewed constructively will evolve and birth a new level of wisdom and understanding.

Reading a book like *Use What's Left* encourages you to evaluate, ask the hard questions, do the hard work, and gain understanding that will prevent another setback.

A setback doesn't have to be fatal. A setback sets you up for success. You can see this by always seeking the understanding of how you got where you were or currently may be and then the knowledge is birthed on how to move forward to where you desire to go.

In this process of seeking understanding, one can easily become overwhelmed. Some people find answers at the bottom of a bottle, smoking marijuana, carelessly sleeping with men and/or women, mindlessly eating, and more just to seek comfort or seemingly escape reality. As we learned in the "Extend and Excel module, nothing grows in the comfort zone. These comforts are only temporary.

When I came out of my fog, I had to shift my paradigm. A paradigm shift is a fundamental element in changing your perception, approach, and underlying assumptions. I presumed prior to my paradigm shift that everyone else was wrong or had a problem—but certainly not me! I used those temporary comforts to cope, so I thought, but it was only pushing me deeper into my denial and further from my deliverance. It was only when I shifted my approach to life through the lessons I have shared with you, that I was able to be prepared for the opportunities presented to me.

I had to understand my choices determined my future opportunities. I had to understand choosing to use mind- and mood-altering substances would hinder or prohibit my growth. I had to understand other people had no power to block my progress. I had to understand it all began with me. I was perishing simply because of my lack of knowledge. When there is no understanding of what's happening in your life, or why it is happening, there is no access to the knowledge that can set you free. Understanding is the bridge that gives access to the knowledge of how to implement the actions needed to create the life you desire.

The two most important days of your life are the day you're born and the day you discover why. That is the understanding that births knowledge. God creates miracles. Remember that you were made in the image of the Creator. The Creator has a purpose for everyone. Designers have a purpose for their designs, and your designer has a purpose for you.

I've been blessed in my career to have all-expenses-paid travel all over the country. I was one of three certified instructors on the planet that worked in my field of expertise as a software consultant.   The question is, why was I able to change the lives of many with my story?

When you surrender to the Creator, you will be exposed to arenas filled with great men and women. The challenges you face are not just for your growth. Although they may have been painful experiences, they were gifts you can use to bless others. It will help others learn from you, so the amount of pain experienced in their growth can be limited, if not avoided. We have all heard that experience is the best teacher. You don't always have to go out and have your own experience to learn. Having embraced the lessons of my past failures drives me to pay it forward to others that may be in a similar situation.

Some of my journey was filled with pain from the past I hope you will avoid.

I understand people don't care how much I know, until they know how much I care. All these modules are for you because I care. Someone cared enough for me and I understand it is my duty to do the same.

When you come to recognize understanding births knowledge, there are three steps to follow to impress the lesson.

- First, sit down and shift your paradigm. Shift your approach of how you are seeing the setback. Be still, don't be anxious, and allow understanding to birth the knowledge.
- Ask the Creator through prayer to quiet your mind so you are receptive to the things coming to you through your new understanding.
- Receive through meditation what He is sending you.

A calm and quiet spirit is open to the revelations a newfound clarity and understanding will create. When we are anxious we can sometimes miss the message. Use these three steps to actively gain understanding in whatever setbacks you are facing. Ask for the greater message in this chaos to be revealed. I understand everything I experienced was for my greater good and for the greater good of all whom I encounter.

At the end of this module I really want you to diligently seek a better understanding of your personal journey.

There are situations and setbacks we all have faced that are very painful to confront. My desire for you is to truly see and understand the purpose of that pain. I encourage you to find a coach or mentor that you can trust to walk with you through the REBOUND process. On this journey, you may not have all the answers because you don't know what you don't know. You may even find yourself in a RUT. RUT stands for repetitive unproductive thinking. Don't allow your situation to keep you stuck. Ask yourself, what am I to learn from this situation or circumstance? Ask yourself, how can I use this failure, setback, or frustration to propel me forward on my journey? There is always a test before the testimony. Having an understanding of exactly what purpose the setback may serve in your life will birth the testimony of how you received the knowledge to overcome that setback.

Steps to Score
When Understanding Births
Knowledge

1. Observe and correct course when necessary.

2. Don't be distracted; be attracted to new endeavors.

3. Resist telling people how to help you.

4. Realize done is better than perfect.

5. Study the greats and model the behaviors that create positive outcomes.

6. Invite your coach/mentor to evaluate your performance.

7. Attend one to three conferences a year in your area of desired expertise.

8. Invest and learn at the level you expect to earn.

9. Attempt to glean education from your failure.

10. Take time to reflect and adjust periodically.

N

If you think down, you will go down. If you think up, you will go up. You'll always go in the direction of your thinking.
—T.D. Jakes

Negate Negativity

In this module, we will focus on negating negativity. To negate means to nullify something or make it ineffective. Negativity is something that is all around us. Each day it is difficult to see the negative impacts in the world. As a person moving toward a REBOUND from your setback don't find it strange if you don't get the overwhelming amount of support you desire from others. You have made a great decision to make the change but the lingering thoughts of who you are remains fresh on your mind and the minds of others.

People find it easier to see who you were rather than support the paradigm shift to who you are becoming. What I will teach you is how to cancel out or nullify that negativity.

First, be very mindful of who you let into your space when you are moving toward the REBOUND phase. As in a game of basketball, you will have opponents in life. You have those who are openly opposed to your new way of thinking because it is uncomfortable for them. Just know that it may be wise not to entertain that negativity because it becomes draining on your journey.

When I was an active drug user, I would do whatever it took to get what I wanted, and I hurt people along the way. I am sure some of you may have done the same, but the key is not to focus on where you were or presently are, but to focus on where you are going. Intentionally focus on the positive changes you are making by keeping those who support you in your space.

There may be people in your family or former friends who participated in the activities from your past. When you make the decision to shift the paradigm, you must understand you can't allow old habits to creep back into your space. Like oil and water, they can't occupy the same space.

Negating negativity is a daily choice made by each of us. Observe the situation and make a decision based on where you are heading. Then decide if this is attracting negativity or negating negativity.

Negating negativity is also a process. It takes time to master this lesson. With unfailing practice, it becomes more of a habit than a hard task. I remember a time when negativity was very easy for me to create and participate in. When I followed the steps of the REBOUND strategy I was able to gain the understanding needed to transform my life. It was not an overnight process. I must stress that this type of change takes appropriate time and focus.

Most of all, it takes commitment and dedication from the person making the change.

I knew that it was necessary to change my address. I was living on the corner of doubt and depression. My new neighbors were frustration and fear. I had to find a new place near the intersection of destiny and hope.

All the time your detractors are responding to you doesn't mean they're hating; they may be relating to the actions that you were exhibiting. I had to learn when the postman dropped off hate mail, I would just stamp it return to sender. That was required to negate the negativity that will come at you; and notice I said that it *will* come at you.

You must activate and elevate the positive. You must transform yourself and begin making decisions about whom you will allow in your circle, especially your close circle. People are in your life for a season and a reason, and some of them are there for treason. If you're moving toward positivity, unfortunately you must let some people go. Yes, it will hurt, but it's necessary to negate the negative and activate the positive. Everyone will not be able to go with you. Not to sound arrogant, but recognizing the choice to REBOUND is personal. You must decide for yourself.

Some people want to remain around no matter what you do. They want to see if you are going to make it. These individuals will try to ride your coattail to success. If you fail, they want to point it out and say they told you so. That's why it's so important to make a conscious decision as to whom you will actively allow in your circle, especially a close circle.

This ride is not for everyone. Others can't see what they can't see, and they can't see what you see unless you show it to them.

Many people surround themselves with yes-men. These are people that don't hold you accountable for your actions and are not even accountable to themselves.

As I stated earlier, the REBOUND phase is not always a positive experience. Sometimes in the REBOUND phase you must get physical so that you can get back from broken. It requires a strong positive attitude to begin to navigate and negate the negative.

When you're the smartest person in the room, Dr. Dennis Kimbro says it's time to go into a new room. Why is that?

It's very simple. You can't grow, be sharpened and polished for success if you alone are the very best. If everyone looks up to you and you become the end-all, be-all, there will be no reason or motivation for you to get better or for you to grow.

Einstein said the definition of insanity is doing the same thing over and over and expecting the same result. Growth requires doing new things, looking at the things you've done in the past, and reconsidering them to see how you can get better.

As I planned a vacation, I learned to weigh the baggage and determine whether I have to pay a fee based on the weight of my bags. If you are a detailed person, you consider that before you get on the plane. You look at what the allowable baggage weight is and make sure that you are within the criteria. That means you may have to remove something or leave something important behind. If you are trying to get to a specific destination, the most important thing is getting there. That may require making sure your baggage is under the correct weight.

The next most important thing is getting there with what you need. Finally, it's getting there with what you want. Consider your needs and your wants in moving forward and decide who and what you're going to take with you. Sometimes it costs more to take more stuff and sometimes the cost is a price that you are unwilling or unable to pay. In life, get rid of the extra weight that can prevent you from being great.

To effectively REBOUND it is imperative that we get rid of negativity. I like to look at it as a lawn full of beautiful grass that has weeds in it, marring the beautiful, emerald site. You must pull up the weeds that are not enhancing your purpose. That is what the negating the negativity is all about. When you negate something, you cause it to no longer have power, purpose, or place over you. Negativity should no longer have power or purpose in your life.

Steps to Score
When you Negate Negativity

1. Refuse to allow old acquaintances to pull you into yesterday's thinking.

2. Do not revisit situations in life that do not move you toward your new goals.

3. Develop a positive circle of new associates.

4. Seek events and opportunities to help you address the fears of your past.

5. Exchange your routines of bad practices to fruitful, productive ones.

6. Invite your coach/mentor to evaluate your performance.

7. Take a vacation just to celebrate your accomplishments.

8. Go on a retreat to intentionally surround yourself with others striving for the same new outcomes as you.

9. Set aside time to meditate and reset your thoughts and approaches daily.

10. Take time to reflect and adjust periodically.

D

It's choice - not chance - that determines your destiny. -Jean Nidetch

Demand Your Destiny

To Rebound means to respond back with another or better chance at winning. When you get a rebound in basketball that means you get the ball again and have another opportunity to shoot and score. The final stage of this rebound in your life is about accomplishing the task you were assigned to do. That is reaching your destiny. Destiny is a place that exists more than just in your mind or some sacred book.

Destiny is where you belong. Regarding each of the stages orchestrating and completing a rebound in your life, I want to take a quick moment to recap what they are in order to reach your destiny.

We started off with R for "Reinventing Yourself." You must work diligently to become who you desire to be every day for you to become who you were designed to be. Success is not so much about what you get, but about what you get to become.

The E stands for "Extend and Excel." To extend yourself means that you will grow and stretch beyond your boundaries. Excel to operate, to grow into excellence so you can achieve success.

The B stands for "Bake it! Not Microwave it!" In today's fast-paced society people want to microwave so they can get things done quickly. The old-school method of baking allows the development of your new life to take its time and become what it was designed to be with the proper amount of heat and time.

The next letter is O, which means to "Optimize Opportunities." True success occurs when you stop being POOR—passing over opportunities repeatedly.

Which brings us to U, which means "Understanding Births Knowledge" and understanding you are not alone. You are the child of the most-high God. You are accepted because he's already accepted you. When you use God and your understanding of what He wants you to do, your success becomes automatic.

The N in Rebound stands for "Negating Negativity," which means getting rid of all the nos and everything negative that will prevent you from attaining the success you desire.

This brings us to the final point, which is the D that stands for "Demand Your Destiny." When you've taken all those steps, you have the right and the responsibility to demand the deliverance of your destiny. To achieve destiny for yourself and those around you, commit to all the lessons presented in this book.

Survivors that have overcome setbacks and have taken the time to extend themselves beyond their comfort zone will be able to apply the rebound strategy with ease. Now, I am not saying it will be easy or come quickly like a silver bullet. However, if you optimize every opportunity you have and rely on the knowledge you have gained through the process, you will build the strength to successfully endure the process.

Once you have made the commitment, put in the work, stayed the course, and started to see the results, I applaud you. More importantly, YOU need to applaud you.

You will begin to attract the resources and resourcefulness needed as you travel toward your Creator-defined destiny.

Demanding your destiny is vital even when you have made the paradigm shift. Life will still throw some challenges your way, but you will be better prepared. You may get knocked down, but remember, you can't lose if you stay in the game.

Trials may seem to get harder as soon as you decide to make a shift in your modus operandi. The more you practice the REBOUND methodology the more resilient you become. You build muscle, character, integrity, and so much more as you walk through the process and learn how to "use what's left."

If you are willing to take a step, even when you are unclear about what's ahead, then you will attract more of what you are seeking. Surround yourself with people who believe in you even more than you believe in yourself. That is the positive energy you need around you at all times.

Be prepared to go back to the drawing board again and again. Remember your destiny is not going to just be handed to you. You must demand your destiny with every action you take in the process.

You may feel like you have tried repeatedly with no success. I am reminded of the story of the bottled cleaner we see in stores all over the country called Formula 409. The creators of this cleaner decided they would create a cleaner that would cut through grease and oil because they were from Detroit, where the main manufacturing products were cars.

These gentlemen had to remake the formula 408 times before finally getting it right the 409th time. They demanded their destiny by being steadfast in their belief. They did not lose because they stayed in the game.

They did not microwave their way to success nor did they take a shortcut in the process. They allowed time and the pressure from failure to drive them closer to their destiny.

I created the REBOUND strategies to help you stay in the game. Never give up on your destiny. Stand and Demand your Destiny!

As you demand your destiny, you must realize that there will be peaks and valleys. When you've been to the bottom there is no place to go but up. When you're at the bottom, if you land on your back, remember that if you can look up, you can get up.

On the way to a championship season in high school, my team and I realized that we must demand our destiny. The interesting thing is that even though it was our destiny, it wouldn't come without demand. We had to aggressively pursue what we desired to become our reality.

You have the right and responsibility to demand of yourself and others what you desire. First, you must understand who you are. Then you must come to an understanding of Whose you are.

The demands don't have to be dark or sinister. They are justifications of what you want to be. If you can't or won't give a verbal expression of exactly what you want, chances are you will never receive or achieve it.

There are core values and morals that guide us. These core values lead us to our destiny. If you are unclear or murky as to what these values are, ask yourself what your specific morals are. Chances are you will not be able to make the type of demands that lead to your destiny if these are unclear.

In fact, demands will be made on you that you will neither control nor enjoy. The key is to be true to who you are and stand for something or else you will fall for everything.

In essence, you must hold fast to the principles of your core values. To be unclear or have a cloudy understanding of what your core values are will lead to indecision, frustration, and eventual destruction.

At some point, you must take a long, hard, honest look and decide what you stand for. Once you grasp that belief, it will be easy to make demands of yourself and those around you.

What you demand of yourself and others may require getting away from distractions. When you surround yourself with people that are not committed to their core values, you will find they have little interest in your core values. In fact, they might be moved by sources that are diametrically opposed to your vision.

Growth demands honesty, humility, maturity, perseverance, willingness to adjust and correct of you and your circle of influence. For you to grow into your destiny, you must insist that those in your circle are consistent with that vision.

At the same time, realize destiny is a direction, not a destination.

The closer we approach our true destiny, the more defined it becomes. That means the core values that affect us must be consistent with what we have accepted as the direction of our destiny.

We are able to encounter new and improved opportunities every day.

Therefore, we must become fully aware of what is required to achieve our destiny and constantly check to make sure we're heading toward that direction.

You must demand of yourself first and then battle against all the things that are in the way of your dream. You must find a balance between yourself and the activities that you engage in.

What do you agree to engage in? It must be something you're willing to become accountable for. There may be places, people, activities, and circumstances that are not related to your destiny.

We find ourselves engaged in them nonetheless; we must become masters of self-discipline. In a sense, we must become selfish in order to demand our destiny. Our destiny awaits us.

The famous French philosopher Voltaire said, "what do I owe to my times, to my neighbors, to my country, to my friends; such are the questions a virtuous man ought often to ask himself." The questions you ask yourself regarding your destiny and the demand for the fulfillment of that destiny are rooted in your core values.

One key is to no longer surround yourself with negative people, and instead, surround yourself with people who believe in your purpose and are willing to work with you toward manifesting it. That includes inspiring, positive-thinking leaders that are engaging in activities guiding them toward their destiny and helping you achieve yours as well. Rid yourself of all that doesn't contribute to that type of growth. Therefore, you're able to demand even more of yourself, circumstances, and situations.

That demand doesn't have to be construed as negative. Instead, it is a positive, aggressive formula that results in success toward fulfillment of your destiny.

Destiny is a place between where you are and where you ultimately want to be. The purpose of "Use What's Left" is to get you back on track and headed toward your destiny. That destiny is a place where you were born to be. It is a place where once you arrive, you will be ordained, anointed, and appointed to be there. Your presence there would not only bless and empower you, but it will bless all those around you. It is paramount you not only demand your destiny, but you do well in that destiny. That is what the R.E.B.O.U.N.D. methodology is all about. When you "Use What's Left" you know what's right.

My good friend Cicone Prince recently wrote a book entitled "Are You Climbing the Wrong Mountain?" In this book, he asks some very important questions that all of us need to ask ourselves. The most important question to me was, "Are you climbing the right mountain?"

In it, he quotes Dr. Myles Monroe, who said the greatest tragedy in life is to finish your course and realize that you climbed the wrong mountain; that you did the wrong thing; that God had a different plan for you and instead you ended up doing something that was not your destiny.

When you finally reach your true destiny, you will positively impact the lives of those in your family and those in your community who depend on you. In order for you to reach your NOW promise, your NOW purpose, you have to begin walking and working on that purpose. When you walk on purpose, your purpose will be revealed if you commit to "use what's left."

Steps to Score

When You Demand Your Destiny

1. Establish what your purpose is and walk in it.
2. Master a new piece of YOU daily.
3. Only allow supportive, encouraging sources in your circle of influence.
4. Create relationships that hold you accountable in a healthy way.
5. Serve and encourage others in their purpose daily.
6. Write and revisit your dreams and goals often.
7. Read inspirational/motivational content   daily.
8. Shift your thoughts from negative to positive daily.
9. Embrace the power of failure as education.
10. Take a risk at least once a month.

Epilogue

I recall the days of my high school championship season. As we continued winning game after game, fighting opponent after opponent, the coach made it extremely clear that playtime was over, and it was time to win.

From the day you are born to the day you know why you were born is the time to fly. The purpose of this book is to give you clarity on your "why." No matter where you are, if you're stuck, or striving, you need to be clear on your why. If you're stuck, it means that you don't have a target to reach. If you are striving, that means that your target is far-off, and you may need to have something that is closer. You may need some additional assistance to achieve optimal clarity to understand why you're trying to reach it in the first place. As an athlete, I just wanted to be put into the game, so I could play. I just wanted to get off the bench and be in the game. I knew that my destiny required that I play.

Are you willing to work on your own REBOUND?

If you are going to bake a perfect cake, you have to do it like my Grandma did. Put all your ingredients on the table, then make up your mind on what type of cake you want. Put the ingredients together in the right combination. Make sure all your equipment is operating properly.

Make sure your oven is pre-heated and that you put the cake in for the right amount of time. When it comes out, let it cool down, then put the icing on; then you have yourself something special and worth remembering.

In the meantime, in between time, you make it delectable, and that's what success is about. Along the way, you just might get to lick the bowl and have a taste of what's to come.

That gives you confidence that you can excel and even if they hate you, you will be able to soar. Fate is the achievement of your destiny. Now, you can demand your destiny and what you demand will expand and become all that you want to be.

When you come back from broken, it's time to use what's left and make a REBOUND to your ultimate life!

About the Author

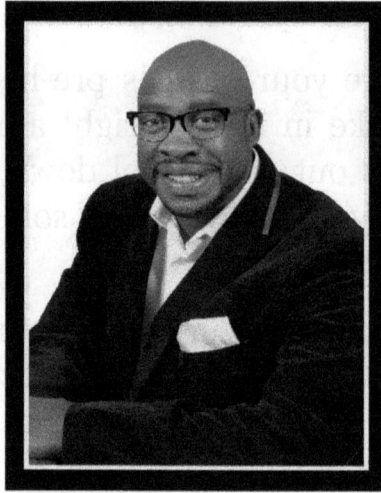

Dr. Ed Womack the "Urban Leadership Strategist," international trainer, consultant, author, radio and TV personality currently resides in Woodstock, Georgia. He was raised on the West Side of Detroit, Michigan. He is a recovering addict with over ten years of sobriety. In 2005, Ed began the journey to overcame being the victim of sexual molestation, numerous bouts of depression and substance abuse.

Womack is the founder of the Man Rise Up Movement and executive producer of the We Rise Media Network.

He serves returning citizens, displaced veterans and individuals finding themselves in a homeless and/or less than optimal season in their life, work, or play.

Womack also specializes in training, conducting seminars, teaching classes and speaking on the topics of purpose, leadership, self-esteem, better decision-making skills and entrepreneurship.

Womack is also the author of three books, including *Back from Broken*. *Back from Broken* reveals the good, the bad, the ugly, and the deliverance from the inner city of Detroit to the program chair for Trinity Community Ministry. He is also the co-author of two Anthologies curated by the Men of Vision: *Reclaim the Flame* and *The Power of Collaboration | New Vision for Victory*.

Through an adaptive delivery of his achievements, setbacks, and his will to re- invent his self; he has a story many of today's male youth and adults can relate to. Taking personal accountability and adjusting to the blows dealt by life's challenges to achieve true destiny is the core theme of this book.

Womack graduated from the Trinity House Men's Program in 2007 and has not looked back since. Womack is living proof that the peaks and valleys can be overcome, with the right information and commitment to self-awareness and dedication to the service of others.

Womack has shared stages with the likes of Dr. George C. Fraser, Les Brown, Dr. Willie Jolley, Dr. Ruben West, Dr. Dennis Kimbro and Myron Golden to highlight a few of the opportunities his journey has made for him.

www.ingramcontent.com/pod-product-compliance
Lightning Source LLC
Chambersburg PA
CBHW070534030426
42337CB00016B/2193